BULLYING

REAL AND LASTING WAYS TO STOP BULLIES, STAND UP FOR YOURSELF AND OVERCOME FEAR

Table Of Contents

INTRODUCTION:

Bullying is no laughing matter...seriously. Many people's lives have been drastically affected or even destroyed by bullying – and the aftermath isn't anywhere near pretty. Reading this, you probably know what I mean by personal experience. Even you or your children may be going through it right now.

The good news is you can do something about it and reading this book is the first step – learning. The more you know about childhood and workplace bullying, the higher your chances of successfully dealing with your or your children's bullies. Yes, you and your children deserve to live life to the full and that includes being free from bullies.

So if you're ready to live a life of freedom from bullying, turn the page now and let's begin.

CHAPTER 1: RYAN PATRICK HALLIGAN

His mother gave birth to Ryan Patrick Halligan on 18 December 1989 in Poughkeepsie, New York. Eventually, his family transferred residence to Vermont. There, Ryan went to Hiawatha Elementary School. Later on, he'd transfer to D. Lawton Middle School.

According to his father John, Ryan was a kid who was quite sensitive and gentle. During his early years in school, he went through some delays in speech and physical coordination developments. By the time he was in 4th grade, Ryan was able to overcome those challenges but still, school didn't become easy to him as it may be for most other kids and he struggled with it. Nevertheless, he'd always be smiling and giving it his all in school.

Ryan's first taste of bullying came when he was 10, brought upon him by a group of insensitive and rude students. They made fun of his learning disorder and passion for acting and music. Initially, John would just tell Ryan to ignore them because it was just verbal bullying anyway. Later on, Ryan went for counseling, which didn't help much. Unfortunately for Ryan, the bullying continued on and off for the next 2 years in middle school.

In 2002, John learned from Ryan that he was being bullied again. This prompted Ryan to ask for a Taebo Kick Boxing set as his Christmas gift. He felt that this would help him defend himself well. John didn't want to accede to his son's request, feeling it may make things worse for Ryan. He wanted to have a talk with the school's principal and handle the situation diplomatically. Ryan, however, protested on the grounds that it will only make things much worse for him, bullying-wise. So he agreed.

After Christmas of 2002, father and son created a system of practicing Taebo in the basement nightly for about 2 hours. When he felt that his son was ready, he strongly told him to don't just go around starting fights. He advised Ryan to use his newly learned self-defense skills to defend himself only when someone physically touched him in an aggressive manner.

In February 2003, Ryan defended himself from his bully. Surprisingly, the bully stopped bothering him after that. In fact, the bully befriended him by the end of Grade 7. Sadly, it was for the wrong reasons. After Ryan shared an embarrassing experience about being examined for stomach pains, the ex-bully twisted it and spread rumors that Ryan was homosexual.

By the time the summer of 2003 rolled in, Ryan was spending a great deal of his time over the Internet, specifically on instant messaging sites like AIM, without his parents knowledge. It was during these times that he started to be cyber-bullied by his schoolmates over his alleged gayness. It didn't end there as it came to a point that he was also verbally bullied about it in class. In one instance, Ryan reportedly left the classroom crying because he couldn't take it anymore.

Ryan, just like other young boys, began to notice the girls and he had a big crush on Ashley. This girl is in his instant messaging contacts whom he considered to be a friend and an ally. Later on, she became a very popular school personality in middle school. In one of their online exchange transcripts, Ashley made Ryan believe that she liked him too, only to publicly tell Ryan to his – and other people's – face that he's a loser. Worse, it was reported that she intentionally deceived him into thinking she liked him, too. Her goal is to gather sensitive information about Ryan, which she publicly shared in her instant messages to many other schoolmates with an intention to humiliate and embarrass him. But John proudly claims that Ryan stood up for himself.

His first hint at suicide came after Ashley called him a loser. He replied to it by saying girls like Ashley make him want to kill himself. It was around this time that Ryan was having online conversations with another boy about his thoughts on suicide and death. They have also been trading information gathered from websites that feature suicide and death, which include painless ways of suicide. When Ryan told the other guy he was already contemplating suicide, the other person retorted that it's about time he did. That was the last time he heard from the online pal. It turned out that the mystery online pal wasn't a mystery one at all: he was an old childhood friend of Ryan's from Poughkeepsie and had only reconnected when they found each other over the Internet.

This childhood friend turned out to be the worst possible friend Ryan could've had at that moment. He was a very negative person who looks at life from a very bleak lens. Often, the two would talk online about how they despise their more popular schoolmates and how those people made both of them feel about themselves. The friend at one point even suggested that if Ryan killed himself, he would really make those schoolmates feel bad – revenge!

Ryan's parents admitted that there were times when he would open up about the things that make him worry and his thoughts about suicide. He even asked John about whether or not he thought about killing himself. John answered honestly that yes, he did at some point but that he's glad he didn't give it anymore thought because if he did, then they wouldn't have been able to enjoy being family. Then the worst possible thing happened.

Ryan Patrick Halligan ended his life by hanging himself in his room in the early morning of 7 October 2003, while his father was away on a business trip and the rest of the family was still asleep. It was his older sister who found him hanging lifeless in his room later on. No suicide note was found but his parents found out the reason for his suicide by accessing Ryan's computer – cyberbullying. Prior to that, they learned that Ryan had scribbled off the faces of the yearbook pictures of those who were bullying him, including the ex-bully who betrayed him with false friendship and started the gay rumors. Ryan's parents thought about filing charges but unfortunately at that time, no criminal law covered such cases.

CHAPTER 2: THE BULLYING EPIDEMIC

"Bullying is never fun, it's a cruel and terrible thing to do to someone. If you are being bullied, it is not your fault. No one deserves to be bullied, ever." - Raini Rodriguez

With the story of Ryan Patrick Halligan, we see just how horrible bullying really is. And it's just one of the millions of stories of how people, both children and adults, are bullied and the damage it wreaks on their lives. But essentially, what really is bullying? Is picking on people enough to be considered bullying?

A bullying behavior is one that's aggressive and thrives on an imbalance of power and repetition. Bullies normally have significantly greater "power" – such as popularity, access to confidential information and physical strength – than the ones being bullied and use such power to harm or control others who are deemed to be less powerful. Such power imbalance however, doesn't have to remain constant and there are instances that it changes or shifts over time, even with the same cast of characters. Bullies also do this more than once or at the very least, has a very high potential and capability to do it over and over should they desire to do so. Intentionally excluding someone from a group, verbally or physically attacking people, spreading malicious rumors and threatening are some of the ways bullying is done on the weaker party or parties.

There are 3 general ways people bully other people: verbal, social and physical. Verbal bullying is writing to or saying mean things about another person, which includes among others threats, taunts, inappropriate sexual comments, calling of name and teasing.

Social bullying on the other hand, involves harming others' relationships or reputation – also called relational or reputational bullying. Social bullying may take the forms of publicly embarrassing another person, disseminating malicious stuff about others, telling others to ignore or discriminate against someone in particular and intentionally leaving someone out of a group.

Physical bullying is when the bully hurts another person's possessions or body by way of destroying or grabbing someone else's stuff, gesturing rudely with the hands, pushing/tripping, hitting, kicking, spitting and punching, among others.

Bullying can basically happen anytime – during or after school hours, during or after working hours and even during or after any social gathering. While most bullying incidents are reported at school and work, significant percentages of it are now happening – and continue to increase – over the Internet, in the streets or in the playgrounds.

According to the Center for Disease Control and Prevention's 2013 youth risk behavior surveillance system, 20% of grades 9-12 students all over the United States experienced bullying. In a similar report by the National Center for Education Statistics and Bureau of Justice statistics, about 28% of grades 6-12 students also experienced bullying. And these are just the reported cases, what more of the unreported ones?

CHAPTER 3: WHY DOES BULLYING HAPPEN?

You may think to yourself, "Who, in their right frame of mind, will even consider the possibility of bullying others?" It's wrong and unfair – shouldn't that be enough reason for people not to bully others?

There are reasons that seem legitimate to bullies, consciously or unconsciously, as to their behavior. For more power or popularity, bullies tend to impose their will on those that they feel are much weaker than them. One thing about bullies is that for all their self-proclaimed "toughness" and "righteousness", they don't take on people who they perceive to be at least equal to them in stature and power. Bullying is always making sure there's a weaker person to bully. Bullies hardly pick on someone they know can whoop their asses. Knowing that, victims of bullying may be the least popular, glasses-wearing, obese, frail, thin, culturally and ethnically unique, religious and homosexual people on the bully's side of the planet.

Bullies often bully others to make themselves feel good about themselves. And in order to continue enjoying such a feeling, the bully needs to perpetuate it continuously for a never-ending rush of power and prestige. So when the original object of bullying leaves, the bully compulsively looks for another one to pounce on in order to keep the feelings alive. And in many cases, bullies are some of the most insecure and sensitive people on earth and that they bully others to feel secure and superior. Aside from insecurity and feeling inferior, people bully others because:

-Vengeance: The bully may have been a bullied victim in the past too, whether by peers or family members. They may have been teased really badly to the point where they may have felt worthless or unimportant. This or similar feelings of being bullied may be their unconscious – or even conscious – way of getting even, albeit on other and weaker people.

-Loneliness: Bullies may also be doing it because they feel insignificant, unimportant, worthless and left out. Everyone needs attention and those who aren't noticed enough may transform into bullies later on. Why? Bullying can give them the feeling that they're significant and powerful, even if they already have friends.

-Domestic Problems: It's not unheard of that bullies are going through rough times at home. They may be experiencing verbal and physical abuse at home, among others, which may be affecting their minds and make them into emotionally aggressive people with fragile minds. In such cases, the bully is a victim as well. Even if they're not abused at home, living with a dysfunctional family, particularly one that lacks openness and affection, contribute to someone becoming a bully.

-Self-Esteem: Many bullies don't have a good view of themselves, e.g., not smart enough, unattractive or unworthy, and bullying makes them feel more confident about themselves. Remember how your mother would tell you to look at less fortunate people to appreciate what you have? In a rather twisted way, that's the case with bullies who have low self-esteem. They make others feel inferior by bullying so they can feel superior and have higher self-esteem.

-Jealousy: As with low self-esteem, bullying makes a bully feel better when jealous of another person who makes them feel inferior or one-upped. This type of bullying may be more specific or particular to a person of interest rather than being generally bullying others.

-Peer Influence: In most cases, bullies like to roll together like birds of the same feather. As such, they tend to become what they are part of. Often times, the desire to hang out with other bullies is for "coolness" or for security, in case the people they bully fight back. They feel stronger and safer when they're in a group of like-minded people.

-Ego: Although many bullies are hurting people themselves, some aren't. They're just proud as hell with egos the size of Texas. They're just so arrogant as to think they're God's greatest gift to mankind and until someone else smacks some sense into their heads, such a belief and behavior will continue to perpetuate.

-Needs To Impress: Part of having a big ego may be the need for other people's admiration. There's really nothing wrong with feeling that way but the problem lies in how to be admired. Bullies normally are void of any special talents or personalities to attract people so what they do is simply push people around – that becomes their special talent or skill, which makes them feel special and admired.

-Unique View Of You: Bullies normally pick their victims based on certain characteristics that they deem as special. Hence, they view their victims as unique or sees them in ways most others don't. It may be that they view their victims' sexuality, physical defects or race as inferior or despicable and hence the aggression towards them. They may either let their reason for bullying others be known or not but it doesn't matter – they're still bullying others and that's wrong regardless.

-Need For Control: Bullies often bully others who they feel are weaker because they have an overwhelming need for experiencing a great sense of control over their lives and by controlling others through bullying, they believe they're able to do that. These people are usually hotheaded and impulsive and people who are not brave enough to stand up for themselves are fair game to them.

-It's Rewarded: Believe it or not, bullying may be a way for bullies to get rewards that are important for them, even if they may not be aware of it. For example, school bullies who often pick on weaker kids for their lunch or allowances receive the rewards of delicious food and money to spend just by intimidating or harassing others. Great rewards for practically no work. The popularity and benevolence often associated with being a bully is another reward that they love to get through bullying. In other words, the behavior is encouraged by rewards.

-Inability To Control Emotions: Some people simply can't control their frustration and anger to the point they resort to hurting other people. With such inability to manage feelings, small incidents and disappointments can cause such people to tick so violently as to react with physical, relational or verbal aggression. An example of this is when a person accidentally bumps into a bully. Even after apologizing, the bully would beat up the other person as a "consequence" of bumping into him.

Bullies may have logical reasons for their behavior but no amount of such will ever justify it. It's a very serious issue that won't just drift away – it needs to be addressed together by the necessary parties such as administrators, teachers, parents, management and government agencies, among others. With the right tools and techniques, victims of bullying can be taught how to handle it well and bullies' minds can be changed.

CHAPTER 4: EFFECTS OF BULLYING

Maybe because of many people's impressions that bullying and being bullied is a harmless part of life or one that is necessary for learning to stand up for one's self, it's significance is often undermined or taken for granted. While some kids can and do stand up to bullying, others can't and don't. They give in to bullying and grow up to be adults with deep and life disturbing issues. Some adults may, as a result of being bullied as such, live the rest of their lives in ways that they didn't use to before – and in negative ways at that.

Bullying doesn't just affect the victim, believe it or not. It affects the bully too.

EFFECTS ON THE VICTIM AND ON THE BULLY

For children, bullying can make them lose interest in studying especially if the bullying happens in school because studying is associated with it – the place where he or she is bullied. As a result, it can lead to serious drops in academic performance and if the academic performance is already poor to begin with, getting kicked out of school or dropping out from it. Moreover, bullying kids may result in physical injuries and mental issues.

Anxiety and depression at such a very young age may also be a result of being bullied. I mean, who wouldn't be, especially if the kid's personality is neither aggressive nor strong? They'll end up sad and lonely and may even experience sleeping and eating disorders on top of becoming disinterested in the activities they normally love to do.

Worse, it may just end the kid's life as with Ryan Patrick Halligan. The media is rife with stories of kids committing suicides as a result of being bullied. Equally bad is the tendency to go the other route – revenge. Many of the school shooting incidents were acts of revenge by kids who were bullied and who wanted to take the power back and get even with their tormentors. Such retaliation is often referred to as "bullicide". If you look at the 1990s, more than half of the shootings were related to bullying – retaliation.

Children who have the tendency to behave violently are often bullies. If they continue bullying others unimpeded or without consequences, it will only escalate because bullying makes them feel powerful and power is intoxicating, making bullies want to up the ante even more. Worse, they may even continue being so as full-grown adults.

Kids who bully others have a higher propensity to:

-Participate in other risky behavior;

-Instigate vandalism and fights, which can cause them to either drop out or be kicked out from school;

-Become sexually promiscuous at an early age with an increased risk for being sexually abused and acquiring sexually transmitted diseases; and

-Grow into spouses that abuse their partners and kids.

Short term signs of bullying

While bullying can cause a number of long term issues that those around the victim need to be aware of, it can also lead to a number of serious issues that need to be resolved as quickly as possible to ensure that they do not become more pronounced with time.

(For the Victim) Depression: This is a big one to watch out for, though it can be difficult to pick up pronounced differences in teens who are already naturally quiet and withdrawn. Depression is more likely to be related to instances of cyberbullying which typically

include more of a feeling of hopelessness and tend to typically last much longer than physical bullying encounters and typically increase in intensity over time as well. Signs of depression include:

- outbursts of sadness as well as anger and irritability that is prolonged.
- A loss of interest in hobbies and interests.
- Apparent apathy towards social contact, even with friends.
- Noticeable, sudden change in habits or patterns.
- Noticeable, sudden change in eating patterns or habits.
- Complaints of exhaustion.
- Expression of feelings of hopelessness, helplessness, worthlessness or guilt.
- A lack of focus.
- Sudden unexplained (or poorly explained) aches and pains.
- A sudden interest in suicide/talk indicating potential harmful courses of action.

(For the Victim) Loss of self-confidence: Belief in one's self is important for long term success, especially for those who are young and still making their way in the world. Having belief in oneself can often make the difference between success and failure. If you notice your child suddenly beginning to experience a drastic variation in their general level of self-confidence, bullying may be to blame. Signs of low self-confidence include.

- They seem to become unreasonably nervous and fidgety in social situations.
- They immediately back down when presented with conflict.
- They adopt an eye catching clothing or physical affectation.
- They seem to take all criticism to heart.
- It is difficult to get them to express an opinion.
- They always seem indecisive.
- They always deflect compliments.
- They give up as soon as things stop going their way.
- They are always comparing themselves to others.

- Their posture suddenly becomes much worse.

(For the Victim) Issues sleeping: Even if they won't discuss it, being aware of your child's sleeping habits can go a long way towards letting you know if they are being victimized by bullies. Roughly 45 percent of children bullied reported issues relating to amount of sleep or quality of sleep while 25 percent complained of persistent nightmares. What's more, this pattern of poor sleep can stick with children for years if not decades. In addition, 75 percent of the time when nightmares persisted for a prolonged period of time, bullying was revealed to be at least part of the problem.

(For the Victim) Issues wetting the bed: While wetting the bed is a relatively common occurrence in children under the age of 7, doing so with increased regularity or after a prolonged period of nightly bladder control, especially in older children, can often be a sign of extreme stress, anxiety or psychological trauma such as that brought on by having to deal with a bully, especially for the first time. Regardless of why the issue is now occurring, it is important to let the child know that it is not their fault and that it is an involuntary reaction. The reason for the bedwetting in these types of scenarios is often linked to the response of taking comfort in food during times of stress which can lead to a change in diet which can also cause the condition.

(For the Victim) Physical conditions not caused directly by the bullying: The stress a person being bullied feels at the prospect of yet another conflict with their bully can be enough to cause numerous physical conditions, not directly caused by any physical bullying that may be occurring. Dizziness, headaches and stomachaches can all be caused simply by the feelings of intense stress that may occur as a result of prolong periods of abuse. As such, a sudden influx of these symptoms, without their maturation into an actual illness should always be considered a cause for possible bullying concerns.

Long term effects of bullying

When not caught in a timely enough fashion, and if the results of the initial confrontations are not worked through in an appropriate manner, those who experience severe enough bullying can experience a variety of long term effects that can have severe, perhaps life long, consequences.

The most common two are anxiety and depression that lasts far beyond the length of the bullying session, eventually becoming chronic disorders that will haunt the victims of bullying for the rest of their lives. Either one or both of these issues can make everything from finding new hobbies, exercising, working and even sleeping difficult or, in severe cases impossible. This also goes for forming meaningful relationships either interpersonal or romantic.

Even those who escape either depression or anxiety oftentimes have a permanently impacted self-image and they may never be able to see an accurate reflection of themselves anywhere. It can also lead to an inability in the victim to trust themselves in any high risk/high reward scenarios likely leading to a less successful life overall.

Post-traumatic stress disorder

While it might seem extreme, enough people have come forward with a variation of complex post-traumatic stress disorder, specific to bullying, that a detailed analysis of just what constitutes it is readily available. Those who are now suffering from bullying related PTSD tend to exhibit the following symptoms:

- Periods of extreme chronic fatigue because their flight or fight response is always active whenever they are in a space that is not considered completely safe.
- A particularly intense need to express vitriolic anger when it comes to injustice either real or perceived.
- An extreme, driving desire to be validated, recognized, understood or acknowledged.

- A strong reticence to avoid talking or thinking about the subject of bullying.
- A strong sense of the difference between justice and revenge with a stong focus on the former over the latter.
- Rarely objective when it comes to slights both real or perceived with a tendency to vacillate between anger and forgiveness.
- Emotionally fragile.
- A feeling of numbness that extends beyond a lack of emotion to a physically deadening of sensation.
- A tendency towards clumsiness.
- A tendency towards absentmindedness.
- A strangely acute ability to judge the amount of time which has passed or the amount of distance traveled.
- An extreme sense of commitment to the environment either locally or on a broader scale.
- A focus on living a healthy lifestyle including the adoption of a vegan or vegetarian diet. Red meat is specifically avoided.
- A pervasive need to justify every thought or action or to prove self-worth when surrounded by friends or loved ones.
- A keen sense of when they are being victimized or betrayed by another person either real or imagined.
- Visions of potentially violent scenarios.
- Unwarranted feelings of being unlovable, unlikeable, worthless, rejected or unwanted.

What's more, they can experience a unique form of survivor's guilt which causes them to not want to report the bully in the moment, despite knowing that it might lead to viable repercussions. Later on however, these feelings lead to a strong desire to act out against the bully, typically couched in a desire to help others avoid future abuse.

The guilt also manifests itself in a hyper advanced sense that others in the world are unhappy which means that the victim of the bullying feels as though they can never be happy as well. This is also seen in their commitment to helping those who are under stress, even if they brought the situation upon themselves. Those with this type of survivor's guilt are also known to particularly identify with the suffering of others. They may also feel extreme and unwarranted negative responses to merit based award.

Both bully and bullied

Those who are both bullied by others and then become bullies themselves are more likely than either bullies or the bullied to end up displaying a wider variety of limitations throughout their lives. Bullying behavior is often learned at a young age which leads to anxiety and depression that is unlikely to improve as they move into the alternate position to the one in which they started. The variety of psychiatric disorders they are likely to express is also much greater than those who were only in a single camp.

These issues include things like panic disorder, generalized anxiety disorder, and agoraphobia. In addition, they were more likely than either bullies or their victims to have harmful thoughts related to self-harm or suicide later in life.

BY-STANDERS (INNOCENT OR OTHERWISE)

Kids who witness bullying live and in the flesh, though they may not be the subject of it, may feel that they're in a dangerous environment and may feel scared, powerless, condemned for not helping the bullied kid or kids or worse, want to do the same to others.

THE SCHOOLS

The schools where bullying continues to run rampant due to either inability or irresponsibility can also be affected by bullying, albeit indirectly. It can suffer from a damaged reputation, it fosters an environment of fear, mistrust and disrespect and its students don't feel secure or even hate it because they feel that the teachers and administration don't give a hoot about them.

CHAPTER 5: BENEFITS OF BULLYING

While it may seem contrary to rational belief, some studies suggest that being bullied can also promote positive growth in those being bullied. While it certainly won't seem that way to start, being bullied as a child can actually help those who are bullied see positive emotional and social development from the experiences.

IT IS NOT ALL BAD

In fact, while it seems that roughly 40 percent of all of those in middle and high school suffered from some type of bullying, a majority of those ultimately end up doing quite fine in life, with some 40 percent of the original 40 percent even going on to do significantly better than the general average. The studies go on to suggest that the over exaggeration of those who do find themselves bullied to the extreme comes from the fact that the smallest percentage of those under the age of 18 who are bullied often create extreme responses instead of shrugging it off as most seem to do. Teens who get revenge in horrific ways or those who take their misery out on themselves are simply an extremely vocal minority.

In fact, a recent study found that, perhaps unsurprisingly, those who stood up to their bullies when pressed, found it less difficult to stand up for themselves when the need arises later on in life. The results of standing up for themselves also becomes more immediately apparent as those who stood up to their bullies tended to be more mature and have a more concrete grasp of the benefits of conflict resolution. Furthermore, it gives them a more well-rounded view of the world as they learn that not everyone is always going to like them despite what may well be their best efforts to influence an outcome to the contrary.

Those who are bullied have an outlet for negative thoughts and emotions

Another surprising finding seems to be that students who reciprocate hostile feelings, and possibly actions, when it comes to dealing with bullies, actually tend to score higher on things like social competence when tested against their peers. When presented with a bully, students have the opportunity to either turn the other cheek, which can ultimately be fruitless, ignore the issue which rarely makes it go away, or they can engage which can create significant social gains when done in front of a group.

This is likely due to the fact that the human brain enjoys patterns, often even going so far as to create them where none previously existed, when applied to relationships, this love of patterns manifests itself in the natural predilection to enjoy symmetry in existing relationships. This means that children will naturally like those who also appear to like them while the reverse is also true. To take it a step further, children them typically project traits they admire and want to embody onto those they like and the traits they hate about themselves onto those they dislike.

As such, those who have an antagonist relationship in their lives more easily learn what type of behavior is morally repulsive and have a mirror by which their negative traits can be reflected in the most effective way possible. Those who experience a tyrannical bully when they are young, have a much more difficult time lording their power over others in the future.

Having a common enemy teaches valuable lessons

Regardless of all other factors, when a group of individuals has an external threat to unite them, they will work together more effectively, remaining happier and more willing to sacrifice personal happiness for the good of the group for longer periods of time. A bully can be this external threat to a group of individuals and as long as the threat is at large, they will find that all other group related squabbles fall by the wayside. The bonds of those who are standing up to the external threat will last far beyond the event in question.

For children, being bullied provides them with the opportunity to solve a real world problem that is at once big enough that solving it will represent a milestone between childhood and the burgeoning world of adult problems and responsibilities. At the same time, the problem that presents itself is still firmly rooted in the rules of childhood, which makes it the perfect symbolic step towards maturation that all children must eventually come to terms with.

In addition, allowing the antagonistic relationship between bully and victim to form naturally as the result of betrayal can provide lifelong benefits, though the initial shock will no doubt be substaintial. The understanding that people are not always what they seem is a valuable lesson to learn and those who learn it at an early age are less likely to be taken advantage of at an older age when the repercussion of such a betrayal are likely to be much more serious than a few hurt feelings.

Coming into contact with this sort of experience will also allow children to determine what sort of person they would like to be in turn because they have a broader view of the possible spectrum of human behavior. Children learn how to be the adults they become by mimicking the behavior of the adults they see around them but also by having negative experiences that show them how not to act in future situations. In fact, the earlier the negative behavior is experienced the more likely that the child in question pivots more dramatically in the opposite direction.

Response is important

Ultimately, it appears as though the response to the bullying, both from the bullied and the bullied child's parents goes a long way to determining how the child will respond to the bullying. This means it is important to never treat the childas if they were the victim of something serious while at the same time not downplaying the issue to the point that the child feels as though their feelings regarding the issue are not valid. It is important to make the child feel as though their feelings about the situation are worthwhile while still providing a positive framework where they can work through the issue by themselves.

CHAPTER 6: BULLYING RED FLAGS

When someone is being bullied, there are many red flags of that being so. Knowing these red flags will help you recognize them better in your children or someone close to you and recognizing these red flags is the first step towards addressing the bullying issue, if any. This is more so that not everyone who is bullied opens up about it and usually just suffers silently inside.

Particularly with children, it's important to talk to them as soon as possible whenever any of the red flags we'll be discussing in this chapter show up because even if it isn't bullying, it may be some other serious concerns like substance abuse or depression. The best way to help children who exhibit these red flags is to talk to them so the root of the problem may be addressed.

RED FLAGS: BEING BULLIED

One of the red flags of potential bullying are injuries that can't be logically, consistently or coherently be explained. Bruises and wounds where the explanations don't seem to add up may be due to other people inflicting it on the person.

Another red flag is lost or destroyed personal items like watches, jewelry or clothing, among others. Especially if the person is known to be quite careful and responsible with their possessions, it's highly possible that someone else is doing it to them.

Frequently occurring feelings of sickness, stomach pains, headaches and even faking such illnesses to avoid going to school or work is another potential sign of being bullied. Bullying may not necessarily be physical but verbal or relational and as such, the red flags are more psychological and psychosomatic.

When your child or someone else that you know exhibits an abrupt change in eating habits, it's a strong sign that something's really wrong. Examples of these would be children coming home from school very hungry and bingeing even if they bring enough food to school. It may be a sign of physical bullying, i.e., the bullies are grabbing their lunches from them.

Other red flags include:

-A significant drop in self-esteem and feelings of helplessness;

-Grades that continue to go down and increasing disinterest in going to school;

-Insomnia and regular bad dreams;

-More frequent destructive behaviors like suicidal thoughts, self-cutting or hurting and running away from home; and

-Sudden apprehension to be in social gatherings and losing friends.

Don't hesitate to talk to a child or a friend who exhibits any of these or other similar symptoms. You just might be able to save his or her life.

RED FLAGS: BULLYING OTHERS

Bullying isn't' just bad for the bullied – it's also bad for the bully. As mentioned earlier, it can make that person even more violent later on and get him into substance and legal troubles. It's best to nip the problem in the bud and the only way to do that is to identify as soon as possible if someone is bullying others.

Some of the red flags that a person is bullying someone include:

-Aggression or frequently getting into verbal or physical fights;

-Belongs to a group of bullies;

-Frequently being called to the principal's office or ordered to stay in detention;

-Lack of accountability, i.e., always blaming others for their misfortunes and problems and don't take responsibility for them;

-New things or extra-money that can't be explained as to acquisition;

-Very competitive; and

-Very conscious about their popularity or reputation.

IMMEDIATE ACTION

As soon as these red flags are identified, the best course of action is to talk to the person concerned a.s.a.p. You shouldn't wait until things escalate to the point that it's either very hard to address or worse, too late. Don't put off what you can do now for tomorrow.

CHAPTER 7: ENOUGH IS ENOUGH – STOPPING CHILD BULLYING

Given the impact bullying has on children and how it can forever change their lives, mostly for the worst, it's important that we are able to address bullying from the grassroots even before it grows into a full-fledged monster.

PREVENTION

Prevention is always better than cure. As such, one of the best ways to stop bullying is to keep it from happening – prevention. There are several ways to do this: awareness campaigns, educating students, punishment system and an anti-bullying policy.

Preventing bullying even before it rears its ugly head can attack the problem on different fronts. Prevention measures can be directed towards fostering a situation where there's zero tolerance for bullying, behavioral suggestions for potential bullies or even giving them outlets where they can pour out their feelings and thoughts that may lead to bullying, and equipping potential bullying victims avoid such situations or themselves prevent it. There are a number of ways that parents can work with their children to ensure that they have a proper idea of what to do when bullied while still not becoming bullies themselves.

Display the appropriate types of relationships: The single most important thing that parents can do when it comes to ensuring that their children don't grow up to be either bullied or bullies is to emphasize the importance of loving relationships as well as the fact that displaying power is not an effective way to gain social status. As such it is important to never use physical power or influence when disciplining a child or else they will learn that it is okay to be overpowered by others, or even worse, that overpowering others is the best way to get what they want. It is important to always encourage open discourse when it comes to solving problems with a child so they learn that the best way to deal with any situation is with words.

Ensure your child enjoys social settings: Children who are loners are more likely to either become bullied or bully others in the long run. It is important to model the idea to your child that being with other people is a natural and enjoyable thing to do.

Be confident: Parents who back down in order to avoid conflict are teaching their children the same thing. While this will result in adults who don't make waves unnecessarily, it will also result in adults who are less likely to stand up for themselves when they are in fact being pushed around unfairly. It is important to only assert yourself when necessary, however, as being too aggressive can easily send the wrong message. This also goes for those who use self-deprecating remarks about themselves, generally as a defense mechanism. Parents who don't have strong self-images will pass along the message that this is an acceptable way to live to their children as well.

Teach your children to assert themselves: It is important that at an early age each child be taught how to assert their rights while at the same time understanding that there are times when the needs of the many outweigh the needs of the few. The key is to teach them how to assert their opinions in an effect way. Consider phrases such as:

- Now it is my turn.
- Please stop what you are doing.
- Keep your hands to yourself.
- That's hurts, stop it.
- Please call me by my name instead.

Try roleplaying: Bullies typically choose their targets based on the response they receive based on verbal threats or name calling. A desired response gives the bully the power they are looking for while at the same time guaranteeing they will continue their assault, possibly more severely than before. As such, it is important to pretend with your child and walk them through possible taunts they might receive as well as appropriate responses for them to reply with.

In this scenario it is important that children understand exactly how bullies operate and how to hide their emotions while appearing to remain in control. Explain that the bully is trying to incense the situation and the best way to win is to not engage and instead work on diffusing the situation as quickly as possible. When practicing it is important to ensure that your child always retains eye contact while speaking in a strong, authoritative tone, practice daily until your child can perform perfectly on cue every time. Providing your child with the right mindset will go a long way to making them a much less likely target for bullies.

Explain the nature of fear: Children frequently have a negative view of fear and find it a shameful emotion. When it comes to dealing with bullies, it is important that your child understands that there is no shame in being afraid, it is how they respond to the fear that is important. It is important to push through minor things that cause you fear in order to grow but fear also lets you know when a scenario or situation has escalated out of control. Instill in your child the importance of knowing the difference and to seek out an authority figure if things look as though they may get out of hand.

Show your child that it is important to intervene when others are being bullied: While teaching your child how to avoid being bullied is nice, teaching them to help others who are being bullied is a strong step towards creating a future with fewer bullies tomorrow than there are today. It is important to encourage them to strive to remove the victim form harm's way before turning the crowd against the bully. As most bullies are motivated by a desire for social acceptance, this reversal will cause them to lose confidence. It is important to, again, stress the importance of contacting an authority figure when the situation requires, safety should always be presented as a primary concern.

Policies

One good way to prepare a school for handling and neutralizing the threat of bullying is through policies that clearly define what bullying is, prohibiting it in school and establishing the appropriate consequences for such behavior. When bullying is clearly defined, it's more easily identified or recognized as it's happening and can be clearly distinguished from motivation, discipline and constructive criticism, which are activities that may be confused for bullying. The policy itself needs to be clear and based on good research to avoid being too broad and general, which may make students and teachers feel uncomfortable to say anything that isn't "nice" believing it may be taken against them as "bullying". For example, if an anti-bullying policy doesn't clearly categorize what makes for bullying, the basketball team's coach may be afraid to pick the best players for fear that cutting off the worst performing ones may become a basis for scorned parents to file a "bullying" complaint.

Another key characteristic that a good anti-bullying policy should contain is the explicit enumeration of major kinds of bullying, i.e., verbal, physical, cyber and social, among others. It is also important that the policy should also include bullying of those that aren't normally considered as "bully-able" like popular students, teachers, staff and other members of the school's administration.

Consequences

A well-written and detailed anti-bullying policy needs to have a set of consequences that are hopefully good enough to dissuade bullies from doing their thing. Having this helps victims know that they'll be treated fairly and securely in order to encourage them to come out and report their bullying experiences. More than just having a solid set of bullying consequences, the policy should be applied consistently and fairly, without fear or favor, in order for it to have any effect on potential bullies.

Home Education

The nature and perception of bullying has changed a lot over the years and while schools can come up with the best anti-bullying policies, it isn't enough because bullying can happen outside of school. The most encompassing way to prevent bullying is within the family. It's because most people's behaviors are shaped at home – what they see and experience in it. If the school says bullying sucks but is a constant regular attraction at home, guess what? The kid will believe his reality at home. Their role models speak louder than school regulations. More than just punishments, which can only go so far, children need role models to emulate and truth is, the home is the best place for such role models.

While it's hard and time consuming to effectively communicate a community than a family when it comes to things like bullying, objections to family education makes it even harder. This is because of the issue of privacy and confidentiality, which makes people resent and reject any forms of suggestion for change. Many parents would simply be too proud to admit if they're raising their children wrong. But if there's no change in the family environment where say, dad bullies mom or brother bullies sister, it will eventually cascade out into the school and the general community.

At home, parents can keep bullying from happening by teaching and modeling. They can explicitly explain to their kids what characterizes bullying and how's it different from constructive criticism and motivating, among other things, and teach them what behaviors are acceptable and unacceptable in the family. And most importantly, parents should reinforce their teachings with action. It's been said that faith without works is dead and parents' actions can either make or break whatever they teach their kids about bullying.

Other Prevention Measures

Appropriate intervention coupled with supervision can go a long way in arresting ongoing bullying's, including teaching and empowering the victims – both actual and potential – to assert themselves. It includes teaching or encouraging victims and potential victims to avoid circumstances where they'll be bullied.

A good example of this would be a kid who's being bullied because he stinks – literally. The reason for his being bullied is simply hygiene so encouraging and teaching him to practice good hygiene can help make the bullying go away and at the same time, increase his self-esteem because doing so will make him more attractive physically and scent-wise.

Consider also a kid who keeps on wearing a Yankees shirt in an area that's predominantly Red Sox. That's a surefire way to encourage others, i.e., the predominantly Red Sox fans, to bully him. By respecting their territory, he avoids being bullied. In cases like this, prudence is the better part of valor.

Then of course, there are situations where the appropriate thing to do is learn how to assert one's self, especially if he or she isn't doing anything wrong or embarrassing. One way is through self-defense, physical or verbal. Many times, bullying thrives in the absence of resistance, like evil does when no good person acts.

BULLYING IN PROGRESS

There are situations that bullying can't be perfectly prevented and so, intervention in an ongoing one is necessary to stop it. Here are ways ongoing school bullying's can be stopped.

School Administration

School administrators and teachers must be cognizant that bullying isn't just limited to the cliché areas such as playgrounds, bathrooms, school buses and hallways – it can also happen through gadgets and online. They should also be able to clearly communicate to the students that there's a world of difference between telling school authorities of an ongoing bullying and merely tattling. Teachers need to be both vigilant and courageous enough to spot an ongoing bullying incident and step in to intervene and stop it, report it and participate in the school administration's investigation of the incidents. Such investigations, however, shouldn't involve both parties – the bully and the victim – jointly participating in meetings as this can be intimidating to the victim and keep him or her from freely telling the truth.

It's not just the task of the school administration to handle bullying – it's also the responsibility of the parents. They should actively participate in any anti-bullying campaigns that their schools are conducting. Without their active involvement, such campaigns simply won't work.

Students must be encouraged to inform their parents when they're being bullied as well as orienting them on ways are being bullied in cyberspace. How can they be encouraged? The school's administration and the students' parents can teach them exactly how to act when they're bullied or when they see others being bullied and encourage them to take action against bullying. Even older students can be younger ones' mentors about how to avoid being bullied on cyberspace.

Encouraging students to ask for help when being bullied may be a challenging task. How challenging? The 2012 Indicators of School Crime and Safety's numbers revealed that in more than half or 60% of bullying incidents, adults weren't notified. Children simply refuse to tell their parents or any adult for that matter about their bullying experiences for several reasons:

-Reporting bullying incidents makes children even more helpless, which is how they already fell when bullied. By not telling adults, they feel that they regain lost control. Reporting incidents, they feel, will make them appear either a tattletale or fearful, which they think will worsen the bullying even more.

-They also fear that bullies may get back at them even more for reporting the incidents.

-Because being bullied is one of the most humiliating experiences ever, children may not be comfortable with their parents or other adults knowing what's being said about them – true or not – and how their being treated in school. Part of this fear may be the parents or adults themselves – that they'll be judged as weak or humiliating for being bullied and not being able to stand up to it.

-Bullied kids may also feel socially rejected as a result of such – that no one really cares for them nor understands them.

-Lastly, social proof is very important for children and they probably fear that reporting bullying incidents will make their peers look at them unfavorably and reject them.

Behavioral Expectations Of Adults

Students should be afforded a learning environment of safety and security. Part of this are coaches and teachers explicitly informing and reminding their students that in their school, bullying is not and will never be tolerated and that engaging in such behavior will result in punishments. Having both the students and their parents or guardians read and sign copies of the school's anti-bullying policy can help both parties truly understand the seriousness of bullying.

For students who are socially awkward, i.e., find it hard to making friends or adjusting socially, the school administration can foster opportunities to do so or give them tasks to do during breaks to minimize the chances of them feeling isolated and becoming fair game for bullying.

Bullied Students' Parents

One of the parents' biggest responsibilities is to regularly monitor or observe their children for bullying red flags. This is because of the reasons I enumerated earlier for children not opening up to adults about their bullying experiences. When they notice one of the red flags enumerated in Chapter 5 manifesting in their kids, they shouldn't just tell them to suck it up and let it go – they need to encourage their kids to openly talk about it with them and be assured they won't be judged negatively for doing so. The more the child opens up, the better the chance the parents and the school administration can take corrective measures to stop an ongoing bullying.

Another way that parents of bullied children can help their kids is by empowering them – teach them how to handle bullying well. The school administration won't be able to completely monitor and rescue their students from incidences of bullying and as such, it's best to equip them to be able to handle it themselves. One of the best ways to do this is by role-playing practices at home where the children can practice avoiding, ignoring and standing up to bullies. Another good thing to teach children is being able to identify friends and teachers who can help them when they're bullied.

Technological Boundaries

Children should also be taught about cyberbullying and not to participate in threatening emails either by responding to such or forwarding them. Parents can do well to add up their kids in their Facebook and other social media accounts and install the appropriate controls on their computers. One way of discouraging them from improper use of social media is by limiting their access at home to a single, family-use computer and placing that computer in a very exposed place such as the living room so they can be easily monitored.

Giving children the latest advanced cellular phones may not be a good idea because they can easily access the Internet through it and take photos and post them on their social media accounts, which can make them fair game for cyberbullying. Any threatening messages should be reported to the appropriate authorities.

Bullies' Parents

The parents of bullies have a very significant role to play in stopping an ongoing bullying. It's possible that their children who bully others are simply not aware or adept at reading social signs and do not know that what they're doing hurts other children as well. As such, they should sit their child down and educate him or her about the implications of their behavior, including possible legal consequences.

Modeling, as mentioned earlier, is one of the most powerful ways to show children that bullying is unacceptable. When children see their parents walk the talk, chances are they won't bully others or stop bullying them. More is caught than taught and action speaks louder than words. Action also reinforces words. When children are exposed to their parents' or siblings' aggressive behavior or if they're too restricted or constricted at home, the chances of them bullying or continuing to bully others are much higher.

Another way parents of bullies can help their bully kids drop it is by looking for and addressing low self-esteem issues. As I mentioned earlier, bullies can also be suffering from low self-esteem. Parents are in the best position to help their children enjoy higher self-esteem. To the extent they're able to make their children feel loved and accepted without having to be popular or accomplished, chances are that the desire for bullying will stop.

Bullied Students

The best option for bullied students is to report any incidence of bullying to their parents, teachers or any trusted adult. Often times, bullying's go unreported for the reasons I outlined earlier. In particular, reporting cyber-bullying to their parents may result in the confiscation of their smartphones or tablets, hence the reluctance to report. Better to be bullied than go offline. The funny thing is that if the parents find out about it from other sources, the more they'll want to take away their gadgets. But if the kids come clean, then the parents will be more open to letting them keep those devices because by coming clean, they're convinced that their child is serious about addressing the problem and that they're responsible enough to report such.

Bullied students should also take into consideration that the best way to handle bullying incidents is to have responsible adults – parents and teachers – handle it. But since even the best laid plans sometimes go to waste, the last resort is standing up for one's self. But regardless, bullying back is not an option – ever. Wrongs can be never be made right by another wrong. When asserting one's self, the best route is to calmly tell the one doing the bullying to stop or just walk away. Physical defense is only acceptable when physically attacked or harassed already and should only be the last resort.

Another way to keep bullying at bay is avoiding being alone. It's because bullies often prey on those that they feel are helpless. When in a group, bullies will have to subdue more people, which they'll perceive to be either a losing proposition that will only lead to humiliation or something that's not worth the effort. Either way, it can go along way in preventing bullying.

CHAPTER 8: A DISCUSSION ON CYBERBULLYING

While traditional bullying is still a major concern, the act of cyberbullying is the current scourge of the schoolyard. From a legal standpoint, cyberbullying is the act of using communication and information technologies to maintain a repeated, hostile and deliberate attack on another person or group of people with the express purpose of causing the person or group mental damage. Cyberbullying is a more prolonged and well-planned version of Internet trolling and is considered distinct from cyberstalking as the motivations between the two are quite different.

Cyberbullying can include one or more of the following and often attempts to humiliate, wrongfully discredit, put down, manipulate, control or intimidate the recipient. What's worse, the cyberbully may not even know their target as the internet is rife with cyberbullies getting behind specious causes that they may or may not think are just. What's more, there are plenty of facets of the Internet that make it much easier for the cyberbullies to attack others without fear of reprisal.

For example, the ease with which a person can remain anonymous makes it easy for the true identity of the bully to remain hidden thanks to things like temporary email accounts, forum pseudonyms and applications which block the sender's information from smartphones. What's more, the online forums, social media platforms and online video game servers that victims both young and old frequent are rarely moderated to the extent that the bullies can realistically expect to be punished.

The continued advancement of technology means that these days, the smartphone is a constant companion for most, if not all, of the population. This means that those who are interested in cyberbullying their victims have direct, unfettered access to do so 24 hours a day, 7 days a week, 365 days a year. This makes cyberbullying potential much more psychologically harmful than other forms of bullying because the victim is deprived of any type of safe space where they do not have to worry about the threat of bullying.

This lack of safety is ultimately compounded by the fact that the attacks occur in an online space where the whole world could potentially be watching. Compare this to a traditional bullying situation where a few witnesses can translate into feelings of extreme embarrassment and the escalation in that arena becomes readily apparent. This can lead to feelings of extreme isolation among victims especially if the feelings about the situation are turned inward to result in self-hatred or shame which, when left unchecked, can end in suicidal thoughts or feelings.

CYBERBULLYING SCENARIOS

Depending on the specifics of the situation, there are a number of options available to those being cyberbullied including changing email addresses and phone numbers. Unfortunately, however, once information has been posted online, it is extremely difficult to get rid of completely, especially when there are others with a vested interest in keeping it accessible. This can take the form of embarrassing pictures or video, both real or manufactured, altering public information about the victim, or even posing as the victim as part of some larger prank or scheme. Another tactic is to instead reveal private personal information that the victim would prefer be kept secret.

The proliferation of social media sites has made it easier than ever for cyberbullies to interact with their victims as today, more than 98 percent of all those between the ages of 12 and 20 are currently connect to at least one social network. What's more, this age group spends more time connecting with their peers online than they do every other activity except for sleeping. This time spent online is not without risks, however, as more than 2 million individuals in this group admitted to being harassed by an activity that constitutes cyberbullying in the past year alone. What's more, the due to the relatively removed nature of the attacks when compared to physically bullying those who see them rarely if ever do anything to discourage the negative behavior.

Despite these statics, those in the 12 to 20 age group are still more than twice as likely as older individuals to share their personal information online. One of the easiest ways to discourage this type of bullying is to spread the message that online privacy should be of the upmost concern to everyone who interacts regularly in an online environment.

HOW TO PREVENT CYBERBULLYING

For those with children, the most important way to prevent cyberbullying to occur is to take the time monitor your child's interact activity to both prevent bullying behavior before it starts. This monitoring should include the websites they are frequenting as well the information and conversations they are having once they have reached their destinations. There are a number of parental security programs that are available on the market which automatically monitors these types of things.

Outside of monitoring, it is important to establish general rules when it comes to the technology that they use regularly regarding appropriate behavior as well as limiting the amount of time they spend interacting with the digital world. It is also important to discuss with your children how to be safe online and how to develop appropriate browsing habits.

Additional tips that are a good idea for everyone to follow include:
- Keep passwords private and use higher security passwords when private information is in play.

- **Keep photos in the PG realm.** Even if the recipient is just one other person you trust, remember once something has been transferred online, you can never know if it has been properly deleted.
- **Take a moment to reflect on the content you are posting before hitting the post button.** An extra 5 seconds now could save you countless headaches later on.
- **Always log out of public use terminals.** Leaving your information on a public computer can lead to countless problems. Be aware of the places you leave your information.
- **Be aware of what's out there with your information attached.** Take the time to Google yourself to ensure that you have a good idea of what others can find out about you online.

CHAPTER 9: DEFENDING YOURSELF AGAINST BULLYING

As an adult, how do you stop someone from bullying you further? What are your options?

DIY

If you're not being physically threatened or blackmailed, among others, you can opt to resolve it on your own first. The following are tips for dealing with verbal bullying by yourself:

Ignoring Your Bully

As much as possible, ignore the person bullying you. This is most especially helpful and wise especially if the bullying is a once-in-a-blue-moon kind. In many situations, bullies are merely trying to elicit a reaction from you and if you don't give them that satisfaction, they may just get tired and move on.

One way to ignore the bully is to avoid him or her. When you see that person approaching you, just walk away to avoid any confrontation. Just make sure that your body language when walking away is that of a confident one and not of fear and trembling because otherwise, he or she just might hound you.

Another good way of ignoring your bully is by concentrating on something else that you're excited about, like your next out of town trip or that car you've been planning to buy in the next few weeks. If you think about something that's more significant, you can divert your attention away from the bully and be able to ignore him or her. Speaking of distractions, you can also repeat a good statement or mantra inside your head or build an imaginary wall around you that can just bounce off any verbal tirades from the bully.

You want a fun way to ignore your bully? Picture him or her in the most outrageously funny and humiliating costume. That should be enough to help you make light of what he or she's trying to do to you. An example of this would be to imagine him or her wearing only an adult-sized diaper and a gigantic feeding bottle – a literal crybaby.

Keeping a positive attitude or mindset is another good way to ignore your verbal bully. While it may be hard to do so when someone continuously tries to bombard you with verbal negativity, it isn't impossible. Just bring to mind your good qualities that will totally trump the verbal bully's tirades against you. It'll also help you to bring to mind the reasons for bullying enumerated in Chapter 3 – this should help you feel pity for the bully instead of fear or contempt.

Being around people who genuinely care for you and who are also positive can help you be confident enough in yourself to simply ignore your verbal bully's tirades. It'll help the insults simply slide off your back. It'll rob the bully of his or her power to affect you and your self-esteem. When you become more confident and at peace with who you are, verbal bullies won't see you as the weakling they think you are. As such, they'll probably just move on to the next victim knowing it's a losing proposition to continue verbally bullying you. Who knows, it might affect him more than you!

Standing Up to Your Bully

There comes a time when you ignoring your bully simply won't cut it, especially if he or she is already beyond logic and reason. It may already require that you stand up to him or her. Here are a couple of ways you can do so:

-It all begins from inside. To effectively stand up to your bully, you must first be convinced that you have what it takes to do so. To this effect, it will be very helpful to use positive self-talk to build up your self-esteem. Tell yourself that you don't deserve this and the bully has no right to put you down. It will also help you that you are loved and accepted by your family and friends and you don't deserve to be treated that way.

-When you're that secure with yourself, you can afford to shock the living daylights out of your bully by killing him or her with kindness. Being kind and nice to a person who isn't can throw him or her off enough to stop bothering you.

-If kindness doesn't work, simply stand up to the bully and tell that person to get off your back and to leave you. Often times, bullies thrive because the bullied person doesn't retaliate and when the victims finally fight back, they're shocked into their senses and leave them alone.

Consider self-defense options

When it appears as though the person who is bullying you is aiming for a physical confrontation, it is important to always try and mitigate the situation as much as possible using words and calm body language. Especially if there are witnesses around, making it clear that you were not instigating the fight may be important depending the severity of the outcome of the fight in question.

To ensure you are always able to make the right decisions, it is important to understand common signs of aggression in others. This can include but is not limited to an increase in the pitch of the voice, either instances of extreme flushing or paleness, fidgeting or general restlessness, excessive staring without blinking, increased in the rapidness or severity of the breathing, muscle tension, shaking, a clenching of the teeth or jaw or excessive perspiration.

More noticeable signs including, walking in a tight circle, physically attacking objects, stamping feet, rapid changes in focus, a change in the tone of the voice, a dismissal of personal space, swearing, yelling or excessive pointing. These symptoms can be exacerbated by talking to the bully in an extremely familiar tone, by making the issue they are mad about seem trivial, by making assumptions about them, telling them what they did wrong, using complicated jargon or acting patronizing towards them.

Up until the point where you begin to feel physically threatened it is important to try and prevent violence for as long as possible. Consider the following specifics when determining if the time for preventing violence has passed:

- Where are the current danger zones and are there any safe zones in the area?
- Assess how in control of the current situation you are, are the other people around you listening when you speak?
- Are the other people exhibiting signs of aggression?

Taking action

If you do decide to take action, it is important to not hesitate once you have begun to act. You will only have a limited amount of time when surprise is on your side, you will want to use that to your advantage as much as possible. According to the law, any person has the right to use reasonable force in regards to another human being in situations that would result in the prevention of a crime or when taking action to ensure the safety of themselves or others.

In this case, the law only states that force that is used needs to be considered reasonable when compared with the threat that it is used to mitigate as seen by the defender, which in this case would be you. To ensure you come out the victor in the case of a physical altercation keep the following suggestions in mind.

Begin on the defensive

The moment the bully steps towards you with the goal of violence in mind, respond aggressively by pushing at them with your main hand and loudly asserting that they back off. While not terribly aggressive, this move alerts those around you to your plight, makes it clear that you are not the aggressor in the situation for potential legal purposes later and conveys the fact ad that you are not going to be the pushover that the bully likely expected you to be.

Aim for the right parts of the body

Excessive force is rarely considered reasonable except when it comes to extremely dangerous attackers, as such it is important that you make the most of every time you connect with the bully's body to take control of the situation as quickly as possible. In situations where violence is warranted it is likely you or the other person which means it is also no time hold back. Start by aiming for the legs, knees, groin, neck, ears, nose or eyes, avoiding instances of permanent damage wherever possible. Your goal should be to end the fight, not cripple the bully.

When selecting the target to attack, it is important to never close the distance between you and the bully just to attack a more vulnerable section of the body. For example, it is unnecessary to try and punch someone in the nose when you are already in position to kick them in the knee. When aiming for joints it is best to hit them from the side, while the groin and the nose respond most effectively to precise, direct pressure.

When attacking the upper portion of the bully's body it is important to try and always strike in one of three ways, with the outside edge of the hand in what is known as a knife position, a strike with the palm of the hand or a knuckle blow if nothing else seems appropriate. The only time you should strike another person with a tightly closed fist is if you are aiming at a soft part of the body such as the throat.

Make it count

If the situation continues to escalate despite your best intentions it is perfectly acceptable to go for the eyes using a scratching, poking or gouging motion. The eyes are a great choice if you are trying to escape as attacking this part of the body will cause maximum pain as well as disorientation which can make escape easier. If the bully continues to advance, a swift strike with the palm of your hand pushing upwards against their nose will allow you to put all of your weight behind the attack, nasal bones are weak and the resulting injury produces a lot of blood, a great diversion if a quick getaway is required.

The side of the neck where the jugular and the carotid artery are located is a relatively wide target that, when struck properly, can temporarily stun your bully. To correctly perform this strike you simply hold your hand out straight with the thumb pointed inward and then jab the thumb and the side of your hand into the side of their neck as hard as possible.

When it comes to the lower body the best point of impact is the knee as it is vulnerable from practically all sides and, when enough pressure is applied to it, will cause your bully to crumble to the ground allowing you to escape or to press your advantage to end the fight as quickly as possible. When it comes to attacking the knee, the side or back will cause the bully to fall to the ground, kicking from the front could possibly hobble them for life.

Extreme scenarios

In situations where basic self-defense moves simply do not seem to be working, consider using your head, knees and elbows which will likely inflict the most damage possible, though not without a little, or a lot of pain reciprocated across your body as well. These three parts of your body are the boniest which means they pack the most wallop as well. It is also important to think about the differences in size and athleticism between you and your opponent. If you are the larger of the two, try and use your weight and reach to your advantage; if you are the smaller of the two, make your extra speed count.

Finally, it is important to not discount the value of things like keys or pens as weapons, though you should always think carefully about using them and to only do so when you honestly feel as though your life is in danger. A fistfight might result in an assault charge, bringing a weapon into play could easily escalate much, much, higher. It is important to always stop the fight as soon as the threat has realistically passed and never press an advantage once the bully has conceded the fight otherwise you might now be considered the aggressor.

Depending on the area you are in, the environment can also offer up a bevy of tools to make the fight easier. Consider using garbage to your advantage or even something as simple as throwing sand or dirt into your opponent's eyes. Likewise, take the time to consider the footing where the fight is taking place, a well-placed push at the right place and time could send the bully tumbling, drastically changing the pacing of the fight in your favor.

There are situations that the bully is more stubborn and aggressive than you can handle and as such, it's time to ask for reinforcement. For one, telling somebody else about what you're going through often helps you feel better and give you more ideas how to neutralize your bully. It also affords you the benefit of being able to receive other people's assistance in handling your bully, making it for the latter to continue.

Asking for help doesn't necessarily mean you're admitting you're weak and incapable. Contrary to popular opinion, asking for help can actually be harder and take more strength and courage. Why? Going against popular opinion takes a lot of guts and courage so the mere fact you're going against it by actually asking for help makes you a strong and courageous person – enough to go against the flow.

Aside from friends and family, you can ask for help from professors, student unions (universities and colleges), counselors, advocacy groups, your company's human resources department, lawyers and law enforcers, among others. There are many options for getting help for your bullying situation. The key is being able to identify who is the best person to ask for help when it comes to your particular bullying situation.

In asking for help, it's best to talk to a person who you trust and know very well because this person can give you the kind of support you actually need as well as wise advise for dealing with your bully that you'll actually consider applying. Anybody can just throw you ideas and support but for accepting those, trust is needed.

If the option you take is to speak with a counselor or a lawyer, it's best to take a trusted friend or family member along with you. If you think you'll be so anxious or nervous to be able to say what you need to say during the meeting, it's best you write down the things you want to bring up or discuss on a piece of paper or email so you will remember to bring them up during the meeting. Don't be afraid, that's why they're there – to help you out.

In case the person you asked help from doesn't seem to take you seriously, believe you or seems to hold back on taking action to help you, don't let that person's action convince you that your concern isn't important or that it's invalid. Simply look for another person to help you out with your situation. Bullying is never something to just sweep under the rug.

Lastly, it may help to consult with a psychologist or psychiatrist in situations where the bullying is affecting you much already. Being a victim of bullying is a very stressful and upsetting situation that can take a toll on your life, particularly your self-esteem, work/education and relationships. If you don't seek professional help, it may continue to significantly affect those areas of your life and make thing worse than they already are. There's no shame in asking for professional help and remember it's important to do so when you know it's already destroying your life.

YOUR RIGHT TO LIVE BULLY-FREE

Remember, all of us have the right to play, study, work and live peacefully without bullying, discrimination, harassment or violence. Being bullied violates your God-given and constitutional rights and as such, it's perfectly ok to take action to address bullying actions against you. It's ok to stand up to bullying.

CHAPTER 10: WORKPLACE BULLYING

Bullying, contrary to popular opinion, isn't just about kids anymore. Truth is, it never really was exclusive to children, although many of the reported cases involves them. It's unfortunate that many people haven't transitioned out of being childhood bullies and continue being so as adults, especially in the workplace.

Many of us are very, very familiar about bullying in schools especially since most if not all major news coverage concerning bullying concerns children in schools, like the Ryan Patrick Halligan case. The good thing about – if you may consider it that – is a result of such awareness, many resources are now available to help combat school bullying such as forums and websites, advocacy groups and celebrity spokespeople. All of these help make the public aware about the problem of bullying in schools and in cyberspace concerning children – concerned enough to take action against it.

Sadly, adult bullying is often taken for granted even though it can be just as damaging or fatal as children's bullying cases. In particular, workplace bullying can be very, very bad as it can affect not just the livelihood of adults but their ability to provide for themselves and their families, if they have. Not to mention, their emotional and physical health are affected too. But unfortunately, the adult who is bullied isn't as newsworthy as children who are because they aren't as helpless as children are.

Victims of workplace bullying know that it's nowhere near easy. Here, civil responses don't work against adult bullies and compared to school bullying, workplace bullying isn't as easy to avoid or escape simply by changing positions, departments or jobs. And nothing can be worse if the bully is the boss himself or herself. Oh, I stand corrected as there is something worse than that – it's that bully bosses are more common than most people think.

Come to think of it, workplace bullying is so taken for granted and it's obvious in the volume of business books not written about it! You go to a bookstore and you see business books on productivity, management, leadership, selling to the wolves but hardly do you find a book on workplace bullying. The subject seems to be a white elephant or a wallflower.

What aggravates this is the fact that workplace bullying is prevalent. In a survey conducted in 2010 by the Workplace Bullying Institute, it was found that 35% of American employees or roughly around 53 million were victims of workplace bullying while 15% reported witnessing such harassment. In the context of the workplace, bullying is defined as mistreatment in the form of threats, intimidation, sabotage, humiliation or verbal abuse that's repeated by at least one employee. Worse, the survey revealed that close to 3 quarters or 72% of such bullying cases were perpetuated by bosses.

THE BULLY BOSS

Compared to the kind of bullying children perpetuate or inflict on other kids, a boss' bullying is often done subtly and in ways that can't be objectively considered as such. While there are the really obvious bully bosses who go on tirades, harass subordinates sexually, blatantly discriminate or throw tantrums and can easily be complained or sued, many more bosses are more deliberate in their bullying as to make them seem their insidious acts are anything but. Because of their knowledge and position, they're able to get away with bullying by making such acts stay undetected or get around company rules and state laws that protect employees' rights. Some are just so plain evil that they deliberately profile employees who are as meek as lambs, who won't probably put up any fight.

Are you a victim of workplace bullying, particularly by your boss or some other superior? The good news is you can start standing up for yourself and fighting back. You can win the battle with these tips on dealing with such kinds of superiors.

Assess The Situation

Before doing anything, you must first assess whether or not the situation is something that you can fix yourself or if it's something that you need to formally complain about or file a lawsuit for. If your boss creates a working environment that's very hostile to you by repeatedly shouting racial slurs, making sexual advances or by physically attacking you, among others, it's possible that your situation is one that requires formally complaining about with your company's human resources department or even filing a case in court. If so, documentation of events is the key and if you have witnesses who are willing to testify on your behalf, that's better! Good news is that most workplace cases of bullying involving a boss are manageable, i.e., you can deal with on your own. As such, there may not be any need for things to escalate to management or the courts.

Compassion And Understanding

While bullying is something that should never be excused or tolerated, most bullies have their own personal issues. By treating them with compassion and understanding, you either throw them off their bullying game and make them want to stop bullying you or you're able to understand where they're coming from and by addressing those issues, you can help that person stop bullying you and others.

Boundaries

You should assert yourself and set personal boundaries – enough is enough. In particular, you should master the art and discipline of saying no to other people's requests, especially those that are already bordering on abuse of grace. The sweet spot is where you're able to go the extra mile at work but make clear to your boss that you're not someone that can be pushed around and treated like a slave. This means you can say no to your boss' request to skip your husband's long-planned birthday dinner celebration in order to finish a project that your boss should've completed weeks ago.

Know Your Boss Well

Many bully bosses, which may include yours, are like the Incredible Hulk, who go ballistic only when stressed or mad and are actually mild-mannered and nice people like Bruce Banner. By knowing your boss very well, you'll be in the position to mitigate circumstances that trigger his Mr. Hyde-ish bullying tendencies and prevent or stop him from bullying you unintentionally in the workplace.

Get Help

If all else fails, don't' be afraid to ask for help from other managers, your human resources department or employee union. If it's that bad, consider asking the advice and assistance of a lawyer. But if the timing is not optimal, i.e., the economy's bad and you desperately need your job, then asking to be transferred may be the best option available.

OTHER WORKPLACE BULLIES

When it comes to workplace bullies who are not the boss, they can be more difficult to spot as bullying is not a concept that most people give much thought too once they graduate from high school. Nevertheless, it is important to be aware of potential bullies to prevent yourself from falling into a negative situation that cannot be easily resolved. Workplace bullies typically make an overt show of excluding someone from a group conversation or event, they withhold information maliciously and at random, undermine their coworkers, pawn their work off on others, constantly interrupt others during meetings, makes crude or belittling comments, or may even resort to simple yelling or name calling.

If you find yourself being affected by these sorts of scenarios, then it is important to take the time to determine if you are the only person who is being targeted by these behaviors. If the potential bully is mean to everyone else in the workplace, seemingly at random then it is likely they are just a jerk and the situation will likely sort itself out. Signs that you may in fact be a target of bullying include:

- You feel as though you are either always tired of have suddenly developed insomnia.
- You feel like you have traditional flu symptoms for several weeks with no change in severity or frequency.
- Your friends and family comment how much you are talking about work related issues.
- You find yourself unable to enjoy leisure time for fear of going back to work.
- You feel as though the issues you are having at work are secretly your fault though you can't say why exactly.

Improving your situation

If you notice the signs that you are in fact being bullied by a workplace bully, then it is typical to first try and ignore the situation or offer up excuses that would also explain away what is happening. It is important to avoid a negative mindset that is frequently brought on by these experiences and to work to avoid the trap of believing that what is going on is your fault as opposed to the fault of the bully in question.

One way to stay positive about the situation is that unlike childhood bullies who tend to pick on the targets they consider weak in an effort to boost their own status, workplace bullies typically target those who they feel are a threat to them and their own career advancement. Remember that if you stick to your guns and work through the situation you will likely be the bully's boss someday which will be all the payback required.

The first step towards standing up to a workplace bully is confronting them about the situation. While this is easier said than done, the following tips can make the initial exchange go much more smoothly. Start by creating a physical barrier between yourself and your bully, such as by raising out a hand to stop them physically. Start by calming addressing the primary issue and suggesting a peaceful resolution. As this is a workplace argument, it is important to keep things as professional as possible on your end. If things do escalate it is important that witnesses, see you as being on the side of rationality while the bully is the one who escalated the situation.

If the bullying continues it is important to start keeping a comprehensive record of every incident of bullying as well as names of witnesses whenever possible. The more information you have regarding the bullying the better, if possible, record audio or video proof as well. If you are not quite sure if you are currently being bullied, keeping a record can also help as well. An unbiased report of the events, when reread after the emotions of the event have passed, can explain much that was initially unclear.

When information is compiled, it is important that you have as many eye witnesses to repeated incidents, as well as your attempts at disarming them as you possibly can. You want to prevent the scenario from devolving into a he said/she said scenario. While it may seem as though you are the only person being targeted by the workplace bully, this is most likely not the case, take the time to seek out the other targets and you can form a positive alliance to take the bully down.

Before you take your case to someone in a position of authority it is important to ensure that you have a case that is thoroughly detailed and that you present a calm, composed tone while doing so. Much of the workplace bully's behavior is likely not visible to management which is why it has been allowed to go on unchecked for as long as it has. This means you only have one shot to shine a light on the bully's misdeeds, coming at the situation while fresh off a bullying session will only make you seem like the unreasonable one, a scenario which benefits no one except your tormentor.

When you present your case it is important to remember to try your hardest not to make your reporting of the situation seem as though it is a form of revenge, be as professional as possible and only provide a possible solution to the problem if you are asked to do so. Prior to presenting your case it is important to take some time and think about how the situation could be rectified to ensure you are able to return to a fully effective work schedule as soon as possible. If, once you have brought your evidence before your superiors, nothing ultimately changes it is important to stand your ground and not ask twice.

Instead, the best course of action if this is the case is to contact a lawyer and consider legal action moving forward. It is extremely important to not take the lack of action in regards to the workplace bullying lying down, it is this pattern of willful ignorance that has allowed the bully to molest others freely for so long.

Recover from the ordeal

Once you have successfully dealt with your workplace bully, the next step will be to recover from your ordeal as effectively as possible to ensure you get back to do the high quality work which made you a target of bullying in the first place. In scenarios where the workplace recognizes that the bullying was occurring, a paid vacation is typically offered as part of a reconciliation package, don't be afraid to take it, you've earned it.

During this period, it is important to consult with a therapist to ensure that there will be no lingering effects from the experience. While it may be difficult, dealing with problems quickly will prevent them from presenting themselves in more serious ways later on. If you find yourself unable to move past the experience in a reasonable period of time, perhaps a change of scenery is in order. Don't be afraid to look for a new job after a painful experience, it might be necessary in order to effectively put everything behind you.

RIGHT TO EARN A LIVING

You have the right to be able to provide for yourself and your family without discrimination, unfair treatment and harassment. If a bully boss is infringing on that right, then you'll have to stand up to him either alone or with other people's help. Don't let him rob you of your right and learn to stand up and fight – and win!

PREVENTING BULLYING IN THE WORKPLACE

When it comes to preventing bullying in the workplace, it is important for the employer to go out of their way to make it clear that the workplace has a zero bullying policy. It is important to ensure that every layer of management is informed as to the importance of this initiative and that while it may seem like a schoolyard problem, in reality it is no joke. Likewise, it is important to instill in the rank and file workers the understanding that it is important for them to say something when they see bullying occur.

When a situation of bullying arises, it is important to deal with it in a strict, efficient manner. The first time a situation of bullying arises will be the ultimate test of the new policy and if it is shown to be ineffective then the entire policy could be in jeopardy. As such it is important that all complains regarding workplace bullying, especially if the bullies are alleged to be a part of management be investigated vigorously. Even if the people who are submitting the reports seem as those they may be less than trustworthy, it is important to give them the benefit of the doubt.

Another good way for businesses to reduce instances of bullying is by eliminating its root cause in most situations which is competition. Businesses that foster a sense of community support one another and grow as a result. Businesses that foster a sense of cutthroat competition eventually run out of employees because they all stabbed one another in the back.

CHAPTER 11: MYTHS ABOUT BULLYING

The bully is always the bigger person: Bullying is always about power and it is typically those who naturally have less of it that feel the need to do what they can to feel as though they have evened the odds. Especially with the increase of cyberbullying, bullies come in all shapes and sizes. When trying to determine if someone is a bully, don't judge a book by its cover, consider the actions that the other person is taking and make your decision based on those facts, not what they look like.

Bullying is a natural part of life: While it's true that most people experience an instance of bullying at least once in their lives, that does not mean that bullying is normal behavior. Bullies are socially deficient in other areas and accepting their existence goes a long way towards normalizing their place in our society.

There is one right way to deal with a bully: While conventional wisdom states that ignoring a bully's machinations is the easiest way to make sure they lose interest, in reality, every bully is different which means that, while sometimes ignoring them will be the appropriate response, other times you will need to turn the other cheek, alert an authority figure, or even fight back. The best approach to start with is to try ignoring their antics, followed by trying to befriend them if appropriate. Stooping to their level should only be attempted when all else has failed as it is equally likely to escalate things if used too soon.

Bullies are always popular: While John Hughes may feel differently, bullies are rarely actually at the top of the pecking order which means the root of most bullying is a desire for increased social status. The goal of a majority of bullying is to establish control over other people, a variation of the traditional social order. While most people who are traditional well liked would avoid stopping to bullying, bullies who are popular are especially malicious as their overall friendly nature can serve to prevent them from facing normal consequences.

Parents have little control when it comes to bullying: While it is well known that children who bullies are frequently abused at home, there are actually a wide variety of ways that parents can influence bullying scenarios. It is important for all parents to enforce the idea that it is wrong to force your will on others while at the same time making it clear that it is important to stand up for one's self in the face of oppression. Falling too far on one side of this line or the other can make it easier for children to either become bullies, or victims.

This doesn't mean that as a parent you need to intervene directly when bullying is involved as this can work against your goal in more ways than one. First of all, it is surprisingly likely for two parents whose children are involved in bullying to get into heated, possibly physical altercations themselves.

There is typically little leeway when children are involved and bullying characteristics could develop in the parent relationship as well. What's more, even if the parent promises to handle the issue, the results could possibly be detrimental to the other child who is simply a product of their environment. Generally, it is best to alert the school and let them handle the specifics.

Finally, it is important to take reports of bullying from your children seriously, making it seem as though their feelings on the topic are valid, before doing what you can to allow the child to handle the situation by themselves first, within reason.

Bullying is more common among boys: With the explosion of social media that took place in the oos, the trend of boys being bullied more often than girls shifted dramatically in the other direction. It is more likely for girls to be cyberbullied while boys who are bullied are still often done so physically. This no doubt has something to do with the way adolescent boys and girls tend to develop a social hierarchy.

Physical bullying escalates from cyberbullying: While to parents, a physical altercation seems much more serious than the few dismissive texts sent back and forth beforehand, in reality, modern teens find more to connect with in the digital world than the physical one. It's a reverse of the old schoolyard standard, sticks and stones can break my bones put words can never hurt me; today however, it is the written word that is likely to last forever in an easily recallable format while a simple broken bone heals and is easily forgotten.

There is not much schools can do to stop it: With the escalation of cyberbullying in the past decade, a vast majority of states, 48 in all, have strict anti-bullying legislation on the books which strictly defines what is and what is not considered bullying and tasks the schools in question to report it promptly. It is the responsibility of the parents to understand their school's policies and to demand change where necessary.

Bullying is akin to conflict: This is a common misconception as to an outsider, the two can seem very similar. In reality, however, conflict occurs when two or more people with mutual animosity towards one another directly interact with one another. Bullying, on the other hand is typically one-sided and continues for a protracted period of time. As such, it is important to consider conflict resolution strategies separately from bullying resolution strategies as one will rarely work to mitigate the other.

When a child is bullied, others will rarely get involved: Here is one instance of things getting better as time goes one as current studies show that a majority of children don't think bullying is acceptable. This means that it is equally more likely that they will step in directly when they see someone being bullied or that they will go out of their way to tell a person in a position of authority.

CONCLUSION

Bullying may be a serious matter but it isn't invincible. Yes, you and your children can overcome it and enjoy your rights to live a full life free from being persecuted by others – free from bullying. But the things you learned here will only be trivia if you don't apply them to your situation or that of your children's. The real value of the things you learned here will be determined by your course of action regarding your or your children's bullies after reading this book. Don't let this book become a mere source of trivial entertainment. Act so that it would've been worth your while.

Knowing is half the battle. Action is the other half. Together, they give you a complete victory over bullying.

Cheers!

SPECIAL INVITATION!

If you liked what you read and would like to read high quality books, get free bonuses, and get notified first of **FREE EBOOKS,** then join the official Xcension Publishing Company Book Club! Membership is free, but space is limited!

You can join the Book Club by visiting the link below:

http://www.xcensionpublishing.com/book-club